W9-BJD-119

When Fish
Go Peopling

Laugh & Learn Books
9 Cumberland Drive
PO Box 1312
Voorhees, NJ 08043
1-800-236-6048

Library of Congress Catalog Number: 95-82030

ISBN 1-886489-07-6

Printed in the United States of America

Cover by Cathy Wang and Jane Arimoto

10 9 8 7 6 5 4 3

When Fish
Go Peopling

Poems by

Paul Borgese

Illustrations by

Cathy Wang

Laugh & Learn Books

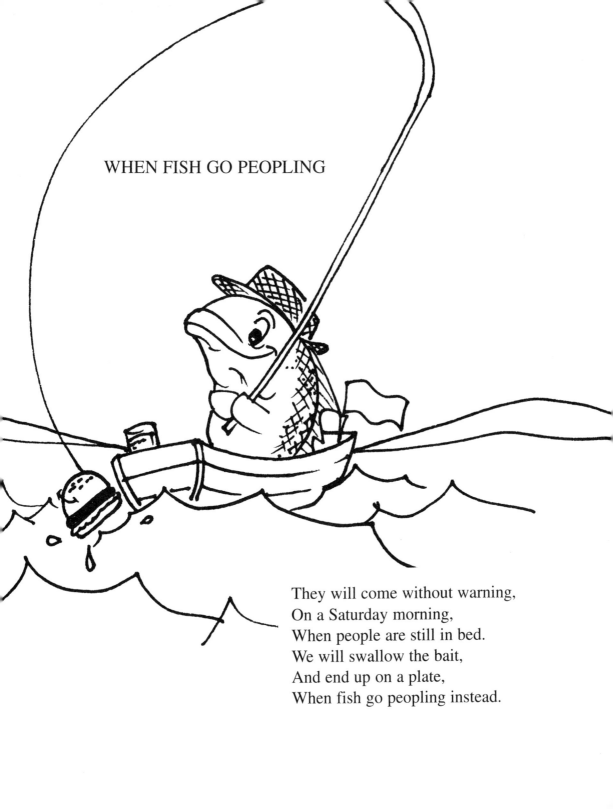

WHEN FISH GO PEOPLING

They will come without warning,
On a Saturday morning,
When people are still in bed.
We will swallow the bait,
And end up on a plate,
When fish go peopling instead.

THE BUBBLEGUM TREE

Across the Marshmallow Mountains,
Down by the Sugarwave Sea,
There lives a very, very old man,
Under a Bubblegum Tree.

He breaks off the branches,
And sticks of bubblegum,
And wraps them up in paper,
That's where we get it from,

Across the Marshmallow Mountains,
Down by the Sugarwave Sea,
There lives a very, very old man,
Who gets his bubblegum free!

THE SAND ONCE HAD A SECRET

The Sand once had a Secret,
That it whispered to the Breeze,
As it whirled away into the Clouds,
Above the Shining Seas,

The Wind blew the Secret to the Moon,
And the Stars heard it as well,
Then it was sprinkled in the Ocean,
When the Morning Stardust fell,

The Waves tossed the Secret back and forth,
Above the Ocean Roar,
And the Sand heard its Secret once again,
From Seashells washed ashore,

It got tangled in the Seaweed,
And in between the Children's Toes,
So it's not a Secret anymore,
Because everybody knows!

Even the Birds are singing the Secret,
Way up in a Sky of Blue,
Just wait awhile, it's in the Wind,
And soon You will know it too!

FANCYFAR

Fancyfar is a magical place,
Deep in the Land of Pretend,
Just follow the Road of Imagination,
And you will find it at the end,

The rivers never stop,
The sun shines all night,
There are balloons that never pop,
And the sky is filled with kites,

There are trees that touch the clouds,
And rainbows for you to chase,
Birds that sing out loud,
And a smile upon your face,

You can visit this magical land,
No matter where you are,
All you must do is close your eyes,
And you'll be in Fancyfar!

WHEN I'M A KITE

Tie some string to my fingers!
Tie some string to my toes!
Take me out on a windy day,
And let me go!

Run into the wild wind!
Run into the breeze!
Let me jump into the air,
And fly me please!

But please don't let me blow away!
Oh, do please hold on tight!
For I would like to fly another day!
When I'm a kite!

SONG OF THE BIRDBATH

The bath shined like a star,
In my backyard,
When the moon danced high in the night,
The wind whispered a word,
To call the first bird,
To bathe in the milky moonlight,

He swirled, splashed, and spluttered,
Like flags, his wings fluttered,
To wave the other birds on,
And in just a bit,
No more could fit,
But they came just the same until dawn,

They joined in a song,
And the wind sang along,
And whistled through the tips of their beaks,
All were excited,
And more were invited,
They hadn't had a bath in weeks,

Without any soap or sud,
They washed away the mud,
Every sparrow, bluejay, and owl,
But away they must fly,
To drip and then dry,
Because no one brought a towel!

WHAT IS A UNICORN?

Did you ever see a unicorn?
It looks just like a horse,
But it has a great, long horn on its head,
And it's magical, of course,

So if you think you see one,
But it doesn't have a horn,
Then it must be some other animal,
Because it's not a unicorn...

MOTHER MOON AND BABY STAR

If Baby Star cries to the Night,
When the Wind should whisper by,
Mother Moon softly sings her song,
With a star-sweet lullaby,

If Baby Star should nod asleep,
To the sound of her twinkling tune,
Mother Moon watches by his side,
Rocking her cradle-crescent moon,

When Baby Star should blink awake,
And shoot across the morning sky,
Mother Moon will smile in the night,
As her Baby flickers by,

But when Old Mother Moon can no longer sing,
The time will come, and that is when,
Little Baby Star will sing to her,
And they will dance in the sky again!

RAINING CATS AND DOGS

We were just on our way to the pet shop,
But I guess we should wait till the rain stops,
Mom says its raining cats and dogs!
So with my umbrella and my boots, I'm all set,
And now I'm going outside to pick out a pet,
Because it's raining cats and dogs!

I USED TO LOOK FOR MIRACLES

I used to look for miracles,
In the clouds of morning dawn,
As I would pick my socks from my bottom drawer,
And slowly slip them on,

In the afternoon, I would search the sky,
I would look both high and low,
I would wander forever both near and far,
Toward the ends of the summer rainbow,

In the night, I would count the twinkle stars,
And call them all by name,
I never quite found where miracles are,
But I would search for them just the same,

But now in my bed, I think to myself,
What was I looking for?
Miracles can be found most anywhere,
Even in my bottom drawer...

THE ESKIMO SONG

I am an Eskimo,
Proud and true,
And I will sing my song for you!

I live in an igloo,
It's an icy dome,
It's not an ordinary house,
But it's my home!

I have a penguin friend,
His name is Awk!
He likes to widdle and waddle,
Instead of walk!

When we're not riding,
On our snow-sled,
We're having a snowball fight instead!

So if you ever see me with my penguin friend, too,
Ask us to sing this song for you!

MARSHMALLOWS AND TEA

I once knew a little girl who was very sick,
And had to stay home in bed,
Her tummy hurt and her throat was sore,
Her nose was stuffed and she was almost sure,
That monsters were banging drums in her head!
"Call the doctors! Call the doctors!"
Her mother and brothers said!

So the doctors came with their little black bags,
And they said, "Oooo! and "Owww!" and "Ohhh!"
They whispered big words and they wrote a little note,
As they checked her ears and nose and throat,
And after they checked her little toe,
They said, "Take this pill and pay our bill!
And then we have to go!"

So the doctors left and the days went by,
Until her little friends came to get her,
"In your bed you have to stay!
You can't go out! You cannot play!"
No, her mother wouldn't let her!
So she slept all day and even all night,
But she didn't get any better!

But the very next day, a little man came,
And his name was Doctor Fiddle D. Dee,
He had a new cure if she wanted to try it,
But she'd have to sleep well and go on a diet,
And eat nothing but marshmallows and tea,
And you can be sure that this was the cure,
Because now she's out playing with me!

BREAD AND BUTTERFLY

As the Butterfly landed on my Bread, I said,
I said as it sat on my Bread,
"I have Strawberry Jam, but I like Butter instead!"
I said as it flapped on my Bread.

As the Butterfly sat on my Bread, I said,
I spoke softly as it sat on my Bread,
"You'd make a beautiful, colorful spread!" I said,
As it pondered upon my Bread.

And then thoughts fluttered through the Butterfly's head,
And with a quickity splutter, he said,
"I don't wish to be spread far and wide across your Bread!"
So he flew fast away off instead!

BEFORE THE LIGHTS GO OUT

Check in the closet and under the bed,
Make sure the monsters have all been fed,
And then make sure that they're all asleep,
So they won't get up and crawl and creep,

Tuck yourself in and pull the covers up tight,
Make sure you can quickly turn on the light,
Then you'll sleep all night without a doubt,
If you do these things before the lights go out. . .

THE GREAT SALT AND PEPPER ESCAPE

Where would they go? What would they do?
Neither of them had a clue,
But they were very unhappy with their tabletop life,
So they planned to escape over fork over knife,

They waited until nighttime when no one would hear,
When the dishes are away and the table is clear,
When the silverware snoozes and the napkins snore,
Then they scampered away toward the kitchen door,

They ran and ran, hand in hand,
And now they live in a far-off land,
Where no one can shake them upside-down,
Or spill their insides on the ground!

THE GRUMBLES

They live inside you in a stomach cave,
Where they grumble and mumble and misbehave,
They talk out of turn and are very rude,
And they are quick to complain if they don't get their food!

I'm sure that you hear them late at night,
When you didn't eat dinner (not even a bite!)
Then they bounce in your belly and stomp with their feet,
They are starving in there with nothing to eat!

They'll sleep without a sound deep down inside,
If your tummy is full, and they are satisfied,
But if you feel tumbles and hear their mumbles,
You'd better eat dinner and feed your Grumbles!

STICKS AND STONES

Sticks and stones,

May break my bones,

I know that much is true,

So I don't take chances,

With boulders and branches,

Imagine what they can do!

WHICHEVER WAY THE WIND MAY BLOW

Said Gentle Wind to Tumbleweed,
"Why do you wander so?
To me it seems that you search for dreams,
In whichever direction I blow."

Said Tumbleweed so lonely sad,
"Oh, Gentle Wind, my dear,
Storm came one day, and I was blown away,
So my home is far from here!"

And then Gentle Wind softly whispered back,
"So do I have a lonely heart,
I am asking you please to follow my breeze,
And my friend, we will never part!"

Through the storms and the sun, they travel the world,
And in each of their hearts, they know,
That in the end, they will still have a friend,
Whichever way the wind may blow...

SEARCHING

Oh, no! Where's my pet bunny?!
Somehow she got out of her cage,
Now I'm on the trail of her cotton tail,
And she just hopped across the page!

THE EXTENSION CORD

It was raining outside,
And I was very bored,
So I decided to follow,
The extension cord.

It went through my legs,

And up the stairs,

Over the rug,

And under the chairs,

Through the doorway,

Down the hall,

I didn't think,

It would end at all.

By the way, I never found the end.
I had to give up with a shrug.
All of a sudden, the lights went out,
Because someone pulled the plug!

THE PIG AND THE PORCUPINE

The Pig and the Porcupine were friends.
They were quite a peculiar pair.
Each night, they would dine,
On foods fancy and fine,
And they would laugh a little more than their share!

They would do ballet through the piles of hay!
They would dance till the night was done!
They would make up a tune
That they would sing to the moon,
And they would smile with the rising sun!

Said the Porcupine to the Pig one night,
"Life is a sweet sip of tea!
Let's dance a jig,
Then pass me a fig,
And sing me a soft melody!"

But the Porcupine cried when the Pig replied,
"We mustn't forget, my friend,
The Farmer will come, we can't be mistaken,
He'll turn you into pins and me into bacon,
And our party will come to an end!"

But then the Pig filled his glass, stood up, and said,
"We will smile and sing to the end!"
And though they were doomed,
The ballet resumed,
And they smiled in the sunshine again!

THE BALL THAT BOUNCED TOO HIGH

When I don't have a friend to play with,
I like to bounce my ball,
I like to bounce it high in the air,
And then wait for it to fall.

Some days I play catch with the birds,
Or I bounce my ball to the sun,
And they always throw it back to me,
It really is such fun.

But once I bounced the ball too hard,
And I cried because that was the end,
The ball went up and up and up,
But it never came down again.

So if you would like to have a catch with the clouds,
Or play a game with the sky,
Just remember this little story,
About the ball that bounced too high.

THE PAJAMA PARADE

Every day after school, we'd make our plans,
Every kid in the second grade,
We decided to meet on Summersalt Street,
To begin our Pajama Parade!

We snuck out of bed at nine o'clock,
Just exactly as we had planned,
We marched down the streets wrapped in blankets and sheets,
With our pillows still in our hands!

But in half an hour, we were back in bed,
Every kid in the second grade,
With a unanimous yawn, we could not go on,
So we cancelled our Pajama Parade!

WHY I WAVE GOODBYE

I wave my hand in the air,
And if you ask me why,
This is what I would say about,
Why I wave goodbye,

I know I'll see you later,
Though I don't know where or when,
So the only reason I wave goodbye,
Is so that I can wave hello again!

Laugh & Learn Books
by Paul Borgese

A Sunday Stroll

Introduce your child to the important lessons of patience and friendship with this classic tale! Your child will accompany Ladybug as she wanders through nature on her way to Centipede's house. Ladybug must decide what to do when she discovers that her friend is not prepared for their Sunday Stroll. Centipede has not even started to put on his one hundred socks and shoes! Wonderful full-color illustrations by Jane Arimoto will dazzle your child's imagination.
The perfect gift for children of all ages!

Hunting For The Whipperwoo

Expand your children's awareness of the world around them so that they can think more clearly and more creatively. Their imaginations will run wild as they explore the amazing adventures of this wonderful beginner's collection of poems by Paul Borgese. Fun for children and adults alike! Features the award-winning poem, *On the Other Side!*

When Fish Go Peopling   *Now in its Third Printing!*

Give your child the opportunity to look at the world through new and exciting eyes. Paul Borgese's best-selling second collection of poems is crafted to improve reading and thinking skills by expanding your child's imagination. Guaranteed to "hook" your child on reading! Includes the award-winning poem, *The Sand Once Had a Secret!*

Coming Soon
from
Laugh & Learn Books

The Spaghetti Confetti Cookbook: Fun in the Kitchen with Rhymes and Recipes by Paul Borgese

More than just another cookbook – this fun-filled guide will introduce your child to the kitchen through easy-to-follow recipes compiled by Helene Borgese and a full plate of poems whipped up by the award-winning poet and author, Paul Borgese. Dozens of fun and delicious recipes for breakfast, lunch, dinner, snacks, drinks, and desserts help children learn about nutrition at home. Each poem adds a dash of fun to the accompanying recipes and will bring your child back to this book again and again. Your child will become a great kitchen helper as he or she learns about safety, nutrition, and even cleaning-up! **FREE BONUS!** Also includes a set of measuring spoons so your child can get cooking right away!

Even the Monkeys Fall Out of the Trees

This long-awaited follow-up to Paul Borgese's smash hit, *When Fish Go Peopling,* promises to be the best yet. Paul Borgese introduces a wonderful cast of characters that your child will never forget. Come meet the monkeys who will teach your child that "everyone makes a few mistakes – even the monkeys fall out of the trees!" Children who jump into this book won't even realize that they're learning important lessons of life – they'll be having too much fun to notice!

About Laugh & Learn Books

Laugh & Learn Books was formed in 1993 with one goal in mind: to create educational books which inspire children to read!

Laugh & Learn Books has pioneered a giving program, **Need To Read**, to benefit several charities that are dedicated to the welfare of our nation's children. Through this unique literacy program, Laugh & Learn Books donates a portion of the proceeds from every sale to a children's charity of the customer's choice, such as **Reading Is Fundamental (RIF)**, a national nonprofit organization which promotes children's literacy.

For more information about the Need to Read Literacy Program, call Laugh & Learn Books toll free: 1-800-236-6048

About the Author

Paul Borgese is the author of numerous children's books including **A Sunday Stroll**, **Hunting for the Whipperwoo**, and his best seller, **When Fish Go Peopling.** He began his writing career in 1986 while working with terminally-ill children as a volunteer at the Children's Hospital of Philadelphia. After receiving his undergraduate degree in English from the University of Pennsylvania, Paul was awarded the prestigious British Marshall Scholarship. He studied literature and obtained his master's degree from Cambridge University in England which is the alma mater of A. A. Milne, the famous creator of *Winnie-the-Pooh*.

Paul has read his stories and poems to audiences around the world. He has been a guest on several radio shows including Kids' Corner, the top children's radio program in the country. He lives in Philadelphia where he enjoys playing guitar for his cat Noche.

Paul is currently completing a new book titled **Even the Monkeys Fall Out of the Trees** as well as **The Spaghetti Confetti Cookbook: Fun in the Kitchen with Rhymes and Recipes**.

Paul's books are available through Laugh & Learn Books. **For a FREE catalog, call toll free: 1-800-236-6048**